LOOKING CLOSE
Teaching kids to love the Earth

[Forests]

by
Sky Stevens

AuthorHouse™
1663 Liberty Drive
Bloomington, IN 47403
www.authorhouse.com
Phone: 1-800-839-8640

Published by AuthorHouse 11/17/2012

ISBN: 978-1-4772-8446-9 (sc)

Library of Congress Control Number: 2012920215

authorHOUSE®

About the Author

As a Canadian author and photographer, Sky Stevens is dedicated to bridging the gap between people and the Earth. Facilitating educational stewardship programs for the Stanley Park Ecology Society in Vancouver and working on projects with The Land Conservancy, Ducks Unlimited, Nature Trust and Naturalists in the Okanagan Valley of BC, led Stevens into entrepreneurship designing and facilitating experiential programs for building self-esteem, trust and teamwork in wilderness settings for children and corporate groups. It was here Stevens recognized how detached humans were becoming to the Natural world. Studying in Oregon, USA, Stevens became a Certified Herbalist to inform and inspire people to embrace the Earth and the interconnectedness of all species. As a professional photographer, currently residing in Red Deer, Alberta, Canada, Stevens uses photography and a passion for the Earth to create children's stewardship books, teaching kids to love the Earth.

This book celebrates every adult who has stood in wonder watching a child explore Nature.

Written and photographed by:
Sky Stevens

There is a forest,
Made up of trees,
Just waiting for,
An Explorer like me.

This incredible place,
Has much to see,
If we look close.
COME EXPLORE WITH ME!

**The forest looks big,
The trees so tall,
I wonder if,
I could count them all.**

What makes the trees,
Grow up so tall?
The sun? The shade?
The rain that falls?

Way up I look,
And then I see,
Brown trunk, green leaves,
That makes a tree.

But looking close,
That's how I find,
Each tree is different,
Like us...one of a kind.

If I look close,
And look with care,
It's the green tops and bark,
The difference is there!

Soft to the touch,
Cedar bark is light brown.
The bows are green,
And hang way down.

If the needles are soft,
And the bark is rough,
It's a Douglas Fir,
And has cones with tufts.

Pine needles are sharp,
Short or long like these.
They grow together,
In two's or three's.

Birch bark is white,
Thin paper sheets.
Leaves drop when it's cold out,
And grow again when there's heat.

As people we don't,
Grow as tall as trees.
But one thing is the same,
We have basic needs.

Most everything living,
Has four basic needs,
Do you know what they are?
Can you list all of these?

Shelter, food, water, space,
Are what all species need.
Plants are the exception,
They only need three.

Plants need water and sunlight,
And room to grow free.
But plants make their own food.
Look close and you'll see.

The roots absorb water,
Nutrients from the ground,
They anchor the plant,
So it won't move around.

Then up through the plant,
The nutrients go.
As they dissolve,
The plant starts to grow.

We call plants "producers",
They produce their own food,
Using soil and water,
There is no need to chew.

How do plants and trees start?
What makes them grow?
If we look for the clues,
Then we will know.

Trees all have seeds,
That fall on the ground.
They don't stay there long,
Seeds get spread around.

Seeds might get eaten,
Or chewed off the cone,
Or blow on the wind,
Or get carried home.

Sometimes seeds get stuck,
In beak, fur or feet,
Or stick on a shoelace,
And end up on the street.

Then seeds just drop off,
Once more on the ground.
If it's wet and there's sun,
A new home they've found

They start out so little.
Much too hard to see.
But if you look close,
There are baby trees!

Look close at the sapling,
That's a baby tree.
It grows and gets bigger.
If you look close, you'll see!

Like us it grows bigger.
Grows tall and gets strong.
Like arms, the tree branches,
Will grow out and get long.

And what grows beside,
This little tree tyke?
Look very closely,
No two plants are alike.

Some are so tiny,
We can barely see them.
And others are large,
With big trunks not just stems.

A forest has layers,
Of plants big and small.
What would an ant see,
Looking up at it all?

Up high are the tree tops.
A canopy of green,
That rises above us,
So crisp and so clean.

Next are the small trees,
Not fully grown.
Competing for sunlight,
They bend when they're blown.

Then comes a layer of,
Ferns and tall grass.
These stand in the shadows,
The small trees now cast.

What's way at the bottom?
Let's look close and see.
There are mosses and small plants,
As small as can be.

And if you look closely,
On the cold forest floor,
Lies fungus and dead leaves,
We've not seen before.

What happens to this stuff?
Plants alive and plants dead?
Are plants someone's food?
Do they keep someone fed?

I will give you a hint.
They might have fur and four hooves.
They might graze in a pasture,
Or through fields as they move.

Perhaps they are fury,
And have lots of feet.
Munching for breakfast,
A morning snack or a treat.

One fact of "consumers"
They eat as they go.
Consumers consume,
Other species to grow.

"Producers" we know now,
Can live on their own.
They make their own food.
Leaving others alone.

"Consumers" are different.
They have to compete.
They rely on producers,
To make them complete.

Sometimes consumers,
Use plants as well,
For homes or for shelter,
Near where their food dwells.

Some of those species,
That like plants the most,
Are lichen or fungus,
Using plant life as hosts.

There are even some species,
That feed on the dead,
Organic material.
They prefer dead, instead!

It sounds kind of creepy,
But, "Decomposers" revert,
Organic decayed things,
Back into dirt.

If it wasn't for these guys,
There'd be no clean space.
With dead trees and debris,
All over the place.

Decomposers, though little,
Have quite a task.
They clean up the messes,
With no time to bask.

Producers produce.
Decomposers eat the dead.
Consumers consume,
Where ever they tread.

Can you see the ant,
As small as a pin?
Ants use the plant life.
And the spider eats him!

It's the cycle of life,
Each depends on the other.
We all have a job to do,
And rely on each other.

So if you're off in the forest,
You know what to do.
Have fun and explore,
But respect each life too!

Remember we all,
Have a purpose and worth.
A special gift,
That we bring to this Earth!

CPSIA information can be obtained
at www.ICGtesting.com
Printed in the USA
LVIW02n2328130813
347720LV00001B

To Order or View
skystevenphotography.jimdo.com
Market Place